The astronauts heard a sharp *BANG!*

The spacecraft quaked and shuddered.

All over the control panel, warning lights were flashing like crazy. Dozens of alarms began beeping at once. Jim Lovell looked at Jack Swigert. Swigert's eyes were wide with fear.

Swigert spoke over the radio to Mission Control in Houston. He had a hard time controlling the shakiness in his voice. "I believe we've had a problem here," he said.

"This is Houston. Say again, please," Mission Control said.

Lovell answered. "Ah, Houston, we've had a problem. . . ."

**The most exciting, most inspiring,
most unbelievable stories . . .
are the ones that really happened!**

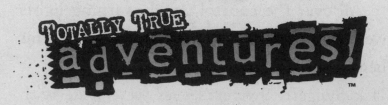

TOTALLY TRUE adventures!

APOLLO 13

How three brave
astronauts survived
a space disaster . . .

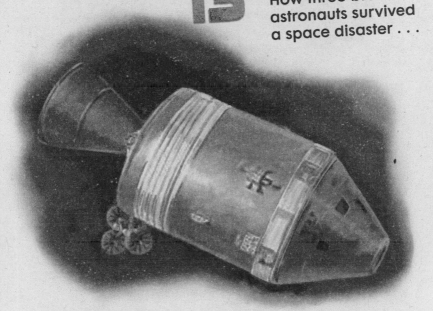

by Kathleen Weidner Zoehfeld
illustrated by Wesley Lowe

A STEPPING STONE BOOK™

Random House 🏠 New York

For my Uncle Richard
—K. W. Z.

My wife . . . Nancy
—W. L.

Text copyright © 2015 by Kathleen Weidner Zoehfeld
Interior illustrations copyright © 2015 by Wesley Lowe

Cover and interior photographs courtesy of NASA

Visit us on the Web!
SteppingStonesBooks.com
randomhousekids.com

Educators and librarians, for a variety of teaching tools, visit us at
RHTeachersLibrarians.com

Library of Congress Cataloging-in-Publication Data
Zoehfeld, Kathleen Weidner.
Apollo 13 / by Kathleen Weidner Zoehfeld ; illustrated by Wesley Lowe.
pages cm. — (Totally true adventures)
"A stepping stone book."
ISBN 978-0-385-39125-2 (trade) — ISBN 978-0-385-39126-9 (lib. bdg.) —
ISBN 978-0-385-39127-6 (ebook)
1. Apollo 13 (Spacecraft)—Juvenile literature. 2. Project Apollo (U.S.)—
Juvenile literature. 3. Space vehicle accidents—United States—
Juvenile literature.
I. Lowe, Wesley, illustrator. II. Title.
TL789.8.U6A697 2015 629.45'4—dc23 2014017578

Printed in the United States of America
10 9 8 7 6 5 4 3 2 1

This book has been officially leveled by using the F&P Text Level Gradient™
Leveling System.

Random House Children's Books supports the First Amendment and
celebrates the right to read.

CONTENTS

ONE GIANT LEAP

On Christmas Eve 1968, the whole world watched and listened. Three American astronauts were about to send a live video from their spacecraft. They were 239,000 miles from home. And just sixty miles from the surface of the Moon!

The astronauts described the gray rocky ground below them. It was so close, it felt like they could almost touch it. But what really amazed them was the view of Earth. It looked like a beautiful blue marble, floating in the blackness of space.

The astronauts—Jim Lovell, Frank Borman, and Bill Anders—were the first humans to fly to the Moon. NASA (the National Aeronautics and Space Administration) was in charge of the mission. They called it Apollo 8.

A little over six months later, the astronauts of Apollo 11—Neil Armstrong, Edwin "Buzz" Aldrin Jr., and Mike Collins—also flew to the Moon. But this time, two of the astronauts, Armstrong and Aldrin, climbed into a spidery-looking spacecraft and took it down toward the dusty surface. Collins stayed in the main spacecraft and waited for their return.

Armstrong landed the smaller lunar spacecraft. The astronauts set up a TV camera, and a billion people tuned in to watch. Armstrong stepped down the ladder first. "That's one small step for man," he said as his boots touched the ground. "And one giant leap for mankind."

Armstrong and Aldrin explored the alien surface and picked up rock samples. They told everyone how easy it felt to walk on the Moon, because the pull of gravity is so much weaker than on Earth.

The astronauts of Apollo 11 were the first to land on the Moon, but they were not the last. Once humans figured out how to get there, there was a lot of exploration to do!

Chapter 1

FLYING TO THE MOON

By 1970, Jim Lovell had spent more hours in space than any other person in the world. Now he was going to walk on the Moon! NASA had chosen him to lead Apollo 13. The crews of Apollo 11 and 12 had landed on smooth areas of the Moon. Apollo 13 would be different. Lovell's team would try to land on one of the Moon's roughest and most interesting areas. Making a safe landing would be tricky. And Lovell couldn't wait to give it a try!

Jim Lovell was living his dream. As a kid, he'd been crazy about rockets. He'd even built a few models that could really fly. When he grew up, he became a United States Navy pilot. By 1968, he was famous for flying on Apollo 8. But he had been part of NASA's space program since 1962.

Ken Mattingly and Fred Haise would join Apollo 13, too. Commander Lovell knew he could depend on his younger crewmates. Mattingly had flown fighter planes for the navy. Haise had been a fighter pilot for the marines. Both Haise and Mattingly were chosen for astronaut training in 1966.

For many months, Lovell, Haise, and Mattingly worked together as a team. Most of the planning for the Apollo missions was done at NASA's Manned Spacecraft Center in Houston, Texas. With help from NASA experts, the astronauts practiced flying to the Moon.

But how do you train for a trip that

few people have ever taken before? You do it through make-believe! NASA called their make-believe missions "simulations" (sim-yoo-LAY-shuns). They built an exact model of the spacecraft. The astronauts got in and pretended it was the real thing.

The spacecraft had three parts, or "modules." The Service Module, or SM, was shaped like a giant can. It held the oxygen, hydrogen, fuel, and power supplies for the trip. The cone-shaped Command Module, or CM, was where the astronauts spent most of their time. This would be their home away from home. When they got to the Moon, a spidery little spacecraft would take two of them to the surface. This spacecraft was called the Lunar Module, or LM (sounds like "LEM").

Every day, Lovell, Haise, and Mattingly climbed into the model CM. They sat on specially made seats, called couches. These were made to fit each astronaut perfectly. In front of the astronauts was a control panel. The lights and gauges on the panel told them how their spacecraft was doing. Joysticks and switches helped them move their craft.

They practiced the liftoff. And they learned about orbiting, or circling, the Earth. If everything went as planned, they would leave Earth's orbit and travel to the Moon. Getting there would take three days. The astronauts learned how to travel safely through the emptiness of space.

They practiced in a model of the Lunar Module, too. Lovell and Haise learned how to fly the LM to the Moon's surface. Haise was a LM expert. He took great pride in knowing more about this module than anyone.

In a nearby room, the Simulation Supervisors, or SimSups, had a devilish task. They had to think up things that could go wrong.

What disaster would it be today? Engine failure? Fire in the control panel? A sudden loss of air? The SimSups could make it happen.

Inside the model spacecraft, alarms would go off. Yellow warning lights would flash on the control panel. The astronauts had to figure out what the problem was. Then they had to solve it, just as if it were a real life-or-death situation. They had two small computers to help them. In those days, small computers were not much more powerful than today's scientific calculators. But the astronauts were never on their own. Officers in Mission Control were always standing by. During simulations, they scrambled to help solve the made-up problems.

One officer was in charge of radioing all the important information from Mission Control to the astronauts. He was called the Capsule Communicator, or Capcom.

Day after day, the astronauts and officers

practiced. The SimSups let everyone know if they had done well. Or if they'd wrecked the spacecraft! In time, they got used to dealing with emergencies. They learned how to think clearly, even under great stress.

As liftoff day came closer, the astronauts moved to the Kennedy Space Center in Florida. They lived in a building just a few miles from the launchpad. Here, far away from family and friends, they could be totally focused. And, even more importantly, they could avoid catching any colds or stomach bugs that might delay the mission.

Unfortunately, that didn't work the way they'd planned. Seven days before the launch, one of the backup astronauts came down with German measles. Since he was only a backup, it wouldn't have been a big deal. But NASA's doctor wondered if the other astronauts would get sick, too. Lovell and Haise had both had German measles when they were little, so they couldn't catch it again. But Mattingly had not. What if he started to get ill in space?

The doctor suggested they replace Mattingly with backup pilot Jack Swigert.

"What?" cried Lovell. "You want to change the crew *now*? A week before liftoff?"

"It's too risky," said the doctor.

Lovell thought Mattingly looked fine. He

asked the doctor how long it would be before Mattingly started feeling sick.

"About ten days to two weeks," answered the doctor.

"So Ken would be healthy at liftoff?" asked Lovell.

"Yes."

"And still healthy three days later when we get to the Moon?"

"Yes."

"So what's the problem?" yelled Lovell. "If he comes down with a fever while Fred and I are on the Moon, he can just sweat it out. I can't think of a better place to have measles than on a nice, cozy spaceship."

Apparently the doctor *could* think of a better place to have the measles! He glared at Lovell. "Mattingly is out of the lineup," he declared.

Of course Lovell was nervous about losing

his CM pilot at the last minute. They had worked together for so long! Swigert had only a few days to practice with his new team. But he was a brilliant young pilot. He had studied every part of the CM. And he was perfectly happy to stay behind while the other two walked on the Moon. Swigert got up to speed quickly. Lovell slowly began to feel better.

Chapter 2

WE HAVE LIFTOFF!

On April 11, 1970, the giant Saturn V rocket stood ready on Launchpad 39A, at Cape Kennedy. When the rocket was fueled up, it weighed six and a half million pounds. The Saturn V was the biggest, most powerful rocket ever built. And every bit of that power was needed to launch the Apollo spacecraft out of Earth's gravity.

The spacecraft sat on top of the giant rocket. The astronauts would ride in the CM for liftoff. For now, the LM was tucked away safely in a small "garage" below the SM.

Altogether, it was a breathtaking sight. The whole thing was nearly forty stories tall!

That morning, Lovell, Swigert, and Haise woke up in their crew quarters as usual. They showered and shaved. They had steak and eggs and toast, just like any normal morning. Then they brushed their teeth and headed to the nurse's office for a checkup. All three were fit and ready to go.

They walked down the hall to the Suit Room. Here, tech assistants helped them into their bulky space suits. In the emptiness of space, a person without a space suit would be in big trouble. His blood would boil. His heart and lungs would pop. He would die instantly. The space suit gave an astronaut oxygen, air pressure, water, and protection from extreme heat or cold. No one could walk on the airless Moon without one. The astronauts liked to call the space suits their "Moon cocoons."

During liftoff, the suits would help protect them if anything went wrong.

A special van took the suited-up astronauts to the base of the rocket. A launch tower supported the rocket. Inside the tower was an elevator. The astronauts rode it to the top. On the way up, they looked down at the flat Florida plains and east to the blue sea.

Tech assistants gave the astronauts' suits, helmets, and oxygen hoses one last check. Then, one by one, Haise, Swigert, and Lovell grabbed the metal bar above the hatch and jumped, feetfirst, into the CM. The techs helped the astronauts fasten their seat belts. And they said their good-byes.

Lovell heard the dull clang of the hatch as the techs pushed it closed behind them. He felt it in the pit of his stomach. This time, it was not make-believe. This time, they really were going to the Moon! But right now, all they had to do was wait. Launch Control had to go through a long checklist, making sure each system was ready. If it was, the officer in charge would say it was "go" for liftoff.

"Launch in T-minus five minutes and counting," the Capcom said.

The astronauts could hear him through the earpieces built into the smooth, close-fitting caps they wore under their helmets. They listened in as the Launch Control officers answered the roll call.

"Guidance?"

"GO!"

"Communications?"

"GO!"

Computers? Engines? They were all "GO!"

At last it was time to check in with the astronauts.

Lovell spoke clearly into his microphone. "We're GO!"

"We're go for launch," said the Capcom.

The astronauts' families and friends were sitting in special bleachers, a safe three miles away from the launchpad. Many people gathered on nearby beaches. Around the world, millions of people watched on TV.

The rocket began huffing and puffing like a great dragon.

"T-minus sixty seconds and counting," said Launch Control. "We're GO for a mission to the Moon at this time."

This was the moment Lovell and his crew had trained so hard for.

"T-minus twelve seconds . . ."

The metal arms holding the Saturn V to the tower pulled away.

"Ignition!"

Five giant engines rumbled and roared.

"T-minus eight . . ."

Huge fireballs burst out from under the

rocket and swirled toward the sky. Everyone watching gasped in amazement.

Four strong metal clamps still held the rocket to the launchpad.

"... three ... two ... one ... zero."

The four metal clamps let go.

"We have liftoff!" cried Launch Control.

The rocket's launch was an awesome sight. People felt its earthshaking thunder as far as ten miles away. But no one on the ground could imagine what it felt like to be strapped inside the CM on top of the rocket.

Lovell told his crewmates to be prepared for the ride of their lives. No simulation could even come close to the violence of a real liftoff. Soon the shaking was so bad, their eyes didn't seem to work anymore. The control panel became one big blur. The noise was so loud, they couldn't hear each other speak.

In ten seconds, the rocket was free of the

tower. At this point, Launch Control in Cape Kennedy turned over control of the spacecraft to Mission Control in Houston.

After one minute and five seconds, the rocket was moving faster than the speed of sound. As they sped faster and faster, the astronauts felt themselves being pressed harder and harder against their couches.

After only two and a half minutes, the rocket's first five engines had done their job. The spacecraft was forty-two miles above the Earth. It was moving at nearly 6,000 miles per hour. The used-up engines were pushed away, or jettisoned, from the spacecraft. The container that held them burned and broke up as it fell toward the sea.

It was time to fire up the next set of engines. The astronauts heard another great roar as the second set of five engines took over. Suddenly Lovell and his crew felt their spacecraft wobble. A warning light showed that one of the engines had shut down.

"Houston, what's the story on engine five?" asked Lovell.

Nobody knew! But somehow they had to make up for the lost power, or the astronauts would be heading back home fast. Quickly, they figured out how much longer the other engines would need to burn. It was a scary moment. But the four working engines did the job. Then they were jettisoned, too.

Finally, a smaller single engine took over. Two and a half minutes later, the spacecraft was in orbit. They were going 17,500 miles per hour, 115 miles above the Earth!

The engine switched off. Everything was quiet. The astronauts looked down at their home planet. They undid their seat belts. They felt like they were floating. And they were! Any little wave of the arm or tap of the foot sent them rolling and tumbling through the spacecraft. That sudden feeling of weightlessness was very strange. This was the first time Fred Haise and Jack Swigert were in outer space. It made them feel a little sick to their stomachs. Lovell told his crew not to worry. They'd get used to it.

"Apollo 13, you are GO for TLI," came the voice of the Capcom.

"Okay, Houston," replied Lovell. "Thank you." His voice sounded calm, but his heart was racing with excitement. "TLI" stands for "trans-lunar injection." "Go for TLI" meant their spacecraft was still in good shape after the launch. And they had been okayed for the trip to the Moon!

With the help of the onboard computer, Lovell aimed the spacecraft in the right direction. The astronauts strapped themselves into their couches. Lovell switched their engine on for one last burn. With a mighty roar, Apollo 13 sped up to 24,000 miles per hour.

It was Saturday, April 11, at 3:48 p.m. From their windows, the astronauts watched as the Earth grew smaller and smaller. Inside the spacecraft, the astronauts didn't feel the speed. They enjoyed the lovely, quiet, floating feeling. They were right on time, and everything was looking good.

Chapter 3

HOUSTON, WE'VE HAD A PROBLEM

The astronauts had named their Command Module Odyssey. With liftoff behind them, they settled into their new home. Outside their windows was the black deadly cold of outer space. But inside, it was a cozy seventy-two degrees. Here they would live and carry out their daily chores for the next three days.

Mission Control told Lovell, Haise, and Swigert that it was okay to take off their space suits. But getting undressed in weightlessness wasn't easy! They laughed as they helped each other unzip and wriggle out of their suits. They bumped into one another and bashed into the couches and walls. Carefully, they folded up their space suits. Then they put on their comfortable white jumpsuits.

The three astronauts hadn't eaten since breakfast. The food locker was stuffed! Before the mission, each had chosen his own menu. There was turkey and gravy, spaghetti and meat sauce, chicken soup, tuna salad, scrambled eggs, chocolate bars, fruit, and more. Each meal was sealed in a color-coded plastic packet. Red was for Lovell, white for Swigert, and blue for Haise.

Dining in space was a whole new experience. First the astronauts shot warm water into their food packets with a water pistol. Next they shook their packets and squeezed them until the food was wet and mushy. Then they snipped off the bottoms of the bags.

The food didn't just pour out like it would on Earth. They had to use their spoons to scoop out one mouthful at a time. Loose food would form into a perfectly round ball. And it would hang in the air in front of them. They could use their spoons to scoop it out of the air. Or they could just float toward it with their mouths open and—*swoop!*—suck it in. Special bags held beverages, which the astronauts sipped from straws.

After meal cleanup, the astronauts had plenty of other chores. The biggest was to get the Lunar Module out of its garage. They had named their LM Aquarius. They attached the top of Aquarius to the pointy nose of Odyssey. This could be a tricky job, but that day everything went smoothly.

The two modules were joined by a hatch and tunnel. Lovell and Haise could open the hatch door and float through the tunnel into Aquarius whenever they needed to.

With this done, it was time for the astronauts to rest. Lovell and Haise floated to their couches. They zipped into their sleeping bags. The bags kept their arms and legs from floating around and banging into things while they slept. One member of the crew would always be awake in case of an emergency. Swigert stayed awake for the first watch.

By the third day, they were closing in on

the Moon. It was April 13, just after 8:00 p.m., Houston time. The astronauts turned on their television camera. They began to send a live video to Earth. Anyone watching could see the inside of Aquarius on TV.

Lovell pointed the camera out the window, to show everyone how close they were to their goal.

"It's beginning to look a little bigger to us now," said Haise. "So far, though, it's still looking pretty gray, with some white spots."

Lovell swung the camera back inside the LM. Haise unrolled a long stretch of cloth.

"Now we can see Fred engaged in his favorite pastime," said Lovell.

"He's not in the food locker, is he?" joked the Capcom.

"That's his second-favorite pastime," said Lovell. "Now he's rigging his hammock for sleep on the lunar surface."

"Roger," replied the Capcom, "sleeping and then eating."

"We might also give you a quick shot of our entertainment aboard the spacecraft," Lovell said. He pushed the play button on a small tape recorder.

As the music played, Lovell drifted toward the tunnel. "This is the crew of Apollo 13 wishing everybody there a nice evening," he said. "We're just about ready to finish our check of Aquarius. Then we'll all get back for a pleasant evening in Odyssey. Good night."

They were about fifty-six hours into their mission—200,000 miles from home—and coasting toward the Moon at around 2,000 miles per hour.

Mission Control went through their check-list to make sure everything was working. One officer noticed that the oxygen seemed to be getting low in the SM's two tanks. This wasn't a big deal. Sometimes the gas in the tanks just needed to be stirred up a little.

The Capcom asked Swigert to switch on the small fans that were built into the tanks.

Swigert flipped the switches and waited a few seconds. Then he switched them off.

Seconds later, the astronauts heard a sharp *BANG!*

Strapped into his couch, Swigert felt the spacecraft quake and shudder.

Floating toward his couch, Lovell felt a thunderclap rumble through his body.

He turned and glared at Haise. Haise was a big practical joker. He loved to make loud noises when his crewmates least expected it. It always made them jump. But this time, the look on Haise's face told Lovell it was no joke.

None of them had experienced anything like this before.

Commander Lovell took his seat. On the

control panel, warning lights were flashing like crazy. Dozens of alarms began beeping all at once. Lovell looked at Swigert. His crewmate's eyes were wide with fear.

Swigert had a hard time controlling the shakiness in his voice. "I believe we've had a problem here," he said to Mission Control.

"This is Houston. Say again, please."

"Ah, Houston, we've had a problem," repeated Lovell. "We've had a main B bus undervolt."

"Roger, main B undervolt," repeated the Capcom.

This could be bad news. It meant a fuel cell was losing power. The three fuel cells in the SM made most of their water and electricity. Without them, they would be in danger.

But what had caused the bang? At first they thought a meteorite had hit them. Then the astronauts heard another *BANG!*

Another fuel cell was going down! They had only one left. It would be too risky to land on the Moon now. Lovell had a sinking feeling. He might never get another chance to walk on the Moon.

Meanwhile, the spacecraft kept on swaying and wobbling. Lovell tried to get it under control, but he couldn't.

Frustrated, he unbuckled his seat belt and floated over to the window. He wished he could go out there and see what was wrong. The CM windows did not give him a view of the SM. But he did spot something that tied his stomach up in a knot. A thin white cloud was all around the spacecraft. And it was growing bigger.

"We are venting something out into the . . . into space," he said.

"Roger, we copy you're venting," said the Capcom.

"It's a gas of some sort," said Lovell.

He didn't say it out loud, but he knew exactly what it was. It was oxygen escaping from one of their tanks. The moving gas was throwing the spacecraft out of control like a burst balloon.

There must be something seriously wrong with one of the oxygen tanks. He floated over to the control panel.

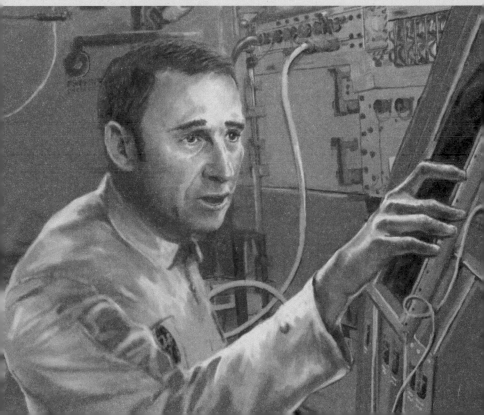

One tank was empty. And the other one was going down fast! The knot tightened in Lovell's stomach. He suddenly didn't feel sad about not being able to land on the Moon. Those tanks were their main source of air. With *both* empty, he and his crew would have only a few hours to live.

Back in Mission Control, everyone began talking at once. What had gone wrong?

"Let's everybody keep cool," said Gene Kranz, the flight director. His voice was calm and steady. "Let's solve the problem. But let's not make it any worse by guessing."

There were four Mission Control teams. They worked in shifts, so there was always a group on duty. Now it was the White Team's turn. They knew they would have to think fast, to save the Apollo 13 crew.

None of the pretend problems the SimSups had thrown at them were anything like this.

For every part of the spacecraft, there was a backup. If one thing failed, there was always an extra one to replace it. They had not trained for what happened if everything failed at once!

Chapter 4

LUNAR LIFEBOAT

"Houston, does it look like the oxygen is still going down?" asked Swigert.

"It looks like oxygen tank pressure is slowly going to zero," replied the Capcom. "And we're starting to think about the LM lifeboat."

"Yes," said Swigert. "That's what we're thinking about, too."

They would have to leave the CM and escape into the LM. In practice, they had talked about this for an extreme emergency. No one ever thought they would really have to do it!

The LM was built to hold two astronauts for a short time. It was about the size of two phone booths strapped together. Its walls were nearly as thin as aluminum foil. But it had its own oxygen, water, and battery power.

Odyssey was going down fast. They would have to leave their Command Module quickly. But first, they needed to save Odyssey's spare battery power. If they found a way back to Earth, they would have to ride in Odyssey for the landing. They would need every bit of power Odyssey had left for the very end of their trip.

The Capcom read Swigert a long list of instructions. Step by step, he began shutting down everything on Odyssey. The oxygen was getting lower by the minute.

While Swigert went through his list, Lovell and Haise moved some of their things into Aquarius. Just two hours earlier, they'd been having a wonderful time, giving the world a tour of the LM.

"I didn't think I'd be back here this soon," said Haise.

Lovell gave a half smile at Haise's little joke. "Just be happy it's here to come back to," he said.

Finally, it was time for Swigert to shut down Odyssey's computer. But before he did, he had to record all the information for keeping track of the spaceship's course. Computers could not share information then, like they can today. If the astronauts shut off the computer before writing the information down, it would all be lost. Swigert read the data from the CM's computer. He shouted the numbers to Lovell through the tunnel. Lovell scribbled them down on a notepad.

All the while, everyone in Mission Control stared at their gauges and held their breath.

Odyssey's oxygen was going down faster and faster. Swigert had only minutes to go. He had to finish reading those numbers! And he had to get them right!

On his notepad, Lovell had to change the numbers, in exactly the right way. Otherwise the LM's computer would not be able to read them. All it took was basic arithmetic. But he was so tired and nervous, he asked Mission Control to check his work. Any error meant they would end up lost in space forever.

"Okay, Aquarius," said the Capcom, "your arithmetic looks good."

Lovell signaled Haise to enter the numbers into the LM's computer.

Once that was done, the two men began to switch on the rest of the power and get the oxygen flowing in Aquarius.

"Okay. Aquarius is up and Odyssey is completely powered down, according to the list you read to Jack," declared Lovell.

"Roger, we copy," replied the Capcom. "That is where we want to be, Jim." In Mission Control, everyone began to breathe again.

Swigert packed himself like a sardine into the lifeboat with his crewmates. Here they could be safe, at least for a while. Maybe they would have enough time to figure out a solution to their problem. If they didn't, they knew they faced a lonely death in outer space.

With all the power down in Odyssey, the whole spacecraft was growing colder. "You know," said Lovell, "if it's getting cold in here, it's going to be freezing in Odyssey. We may want to bring some food and water over here."

"You want me to get it?" asked Swigert.

"It would be a big help," said Lovell. "Fill up as many drink bags as you can with water, and grab some food packets along with them."

"I'm on my way," replied Swigert. Standing

on the engine cover in the center of the LM, Swigert bent his knees and pushed off. The jump sent him straight through the tunnel.

He stopped at the food locker and scooped up a few handfuls of food packets. He grabbed a few of the drink bags and began to fill them with the water gun. On the first bag, Swigert fired the gun too soon. A perfectly round silvery ball of water escaped. It floated slowly

toward Swigert's foot. Swigert cringed as it splashed against one of his cloth shoes.

"Argh!" he shouted.

"What's wrong?" called Haise.

"Nothing. I just drenched my shoes."

"They'll dry," said Haise.

"They'll freeze before they dry," groaned Swigert. His feet felt cold already.

Chapter 5

THE BEST WAY HOME

Besides eating and drinking, breathing and staying warm, there was one big question on everyone's minds: *what's the best way home?* Should they turn around and head back to Earth? Or would it be better to loop around the Moon first?

They were already speeding toward the Moon. To suddenly stop and go the other way would take a lot of energy. Their SM engine could do the job. But they probably didn't have enough battery power left to turn it on. Even worse, the explosion could have damaged the engine. Turning it on might send the spacecraft tumbling out of control.

Looping around the Moon would mean traveling farther. But the gravity of the Moon would give them a speed boost. It would fling them fast, like a pebble slung from a slingshot. But they needed a working engine. No one had ever thought of flying the whole spacecraft with just the LM's small engine. Now that was exactly what they were going to have to do!

Mission Control called Ken Mattingly. He'd been moping around at home, waiting to get the measles. Now his crew needed him! He and another Apollo astronaut, John Young, went into the simulator. They tried out ways to help Apollo 13. Mattingly and Young would make sure whatever they told the crew to do would actually work.

Lovell's job would be to get his spacecraft

into orbit around the Moon. To do that, he had to aim it in the right direction. If their aim was off, they could zoom past the Moon instead of looping around it.

Normally, the computer would tell the astronauts exactly where they were. But Lovell was still worried. Had he really gotten those numbers right earlier?

Lovell wanted to check their position with his own eyes. He knew how to find his way, using the stars. But bits of junk from the explosions glinted in the sunlight all around the ship. The bits looked just like stars. There was no way to tell a real star from a "false star."

Lovell sighed. "We're going to have to go with what we've got," he told his crew. "Let's hope it's good enough."

Mission Control agreed. They read the LM's computer and told the astronauts which way to turn. Haise punched in the data.

The LM's thrusters fired. Ever so slowly, the spacecraft turned.

"Aquarius," said the Capcom, "you're go for the burn."

On April 14, at 2:43 a.m., Houston time, the astronauts felt the LM's main engine spring to life. Mission Control officers figured the engine would have to burn for exactly thirty seconds. No more, no less. Any error could send the astronauts off course.

Lovell stared at the control panel. Everything seemed to be working okay.

"Looking good," said the Capcom.

Lovell's eyes moved from the control panel to his wristwatch and back again. Ten seconds. Twenty seconds. Thirty seconds. Lovell held his breath. Then, a second later than planned, the computer shut the engine down.

When the Mission Control officers looked at their computer screens, they could hardly believe their eyes. Aquarius was right on course.

Everyone took a deep breath and got ready for the next challenge!

Chapter 6

THE DARK SIDE OF THE MOON

The doctor down in Mission Control was getting worried about the astronauts. They hadn't had a wink of sleep in over twenty-four hours. People need at least five or six hours of sleep each day. Without it, the astronauts would be in much greater danger of making a serious, even deadly, mistake.

The doctor ordered Haise to bed first. Lovell and Swigert would keep watch.

Haise floated through the tunnel to Odyssey. Enough air came through the tunnel from Aquarius to make it livable. But he was stunned by how cold and lifeless it felt. He could see his breath, as if he were outdoors on a frosty winter day. He zipped himself into his thin sleeping bag and settled into his couch. He lay awake—shivering.

The radio connection with Mission Control became crackly. Haise listened to everyone shouting through the static. After two hours, he returned to the LM.

Lovell looked at his watch. "That's it?" he asked.

"It's too cold up there," said Haise. He grabbed a food packet. "Too cold. And too noisy. You guys can give it a try. But I wouldn't count on getting much rest."

On the ground, the Gold Team would soon take over. Lovell hoped they were more rested than he was. As it turned out, none of the teams were getting much rest. They would grab quick naps whenever they could. But no one was thinking about going home.

In fifteen hours, the spacecraft would slip around the back of the Moon. While they were on the far side, their radio signals could not reach Earth. They would have no way of talking to Mission Control. In the meantime, they had a big problem to solve.

At the rate they were going, it would be ninety-one hours before they reached Earth. The LM was not made for such a long trip. It could hold two astronauts for forty-eight hours. Now it had to hold three astronauts for almost twice that time!

Water was the biggest problem. The astronauts had to drink water, of course. But it was also needed for cooling the spacecraft's many systems. If any system overheated, it would burn out and shut down. Lovell knew they would need to speed up this trip somehow.

Everyone agreed that as soon as they came out from behind the Moon, they would have to fire the LM's engine again. But they had to figure out how to do it now, while they could still talk to Mission Control.

The Gold Team Capcom radioed up the plan. They would have to run the LM's engine for four and a half minutes.

The first step would be to make sure the spacecraft's aim was okay. This burn would be much longer than the first one. So making sure the spacecraft was aimed perfectly was even more important now. And it would be trickier. Any little error could send them hopelessly off course.

How could Lovell check that the LM's computer still knew where they were? Normally, he could just use his own eyes. But those sparkly bits of junk still floated around the spacecraft. He couldn't see any familiar stars.

Mission Control decided Lovell could use the Sun as a marker. That was the one star he *could* see!

Since the Sun was a big target, it might not be a very good test. But it would have to do. Lovell would tell the computer to zero in on the upper-right corner of the Sun. Swigert and Haise would use the telescope to make sure the computer got it right.

Lovell gave the computer the command to do a Sun check. The LM's thrusters turned the craft.

"You see anything yet, Jack?" Lovell asked.

"Nothing," said Swigert.

You could hear a pin drop in Mission Control. Everyone was listening.

Finally, Swigert spotted something. "We've got a Sun!" he cried.

A thin beam of sunlight touched the instrument panel.

Haise peered through his telescope. "Just about there!" he called.

"What have you got?" cried Lovell.

Haise slowly pulled back from the telescope. He flashed his crewmates a huge grin. "Upper-right corner of the Sun!"

"We've got it!" Lovell shouted. He pumped his fist in the air.

"We're hot!" cried Haise.

A huge whoop went up in Mission Control. The officers leapt from their chairs and cheered. The Gold Team's flight director just smiled. He knew he should get his crew back under control. But for the moment, he enjoyed the celebration.

The computer could still be trusted. But in the back of the flight director's mind was a big worry. No one knew if Aquarius's engine would even *start* a second time. It had been built to fire only once.

The White Team entered the control room.
They went over the plans with the astronauts
one more time.

"Aquarius, Houston," said the Capcom.

"Go ahead, Houston."

"Okay, Jim, we have a little over two minutes until loss of signal. And everything is
looking good here."

"Roger," said Lovell. "See you on the other side."

It was Tuesday, April 14. At 6:15 p.m., Houston time, radio contact was lost.

Lovell, Haise, and Swigert stared down at the side of the Moon that always faces away from Earth. Only a few astronauts had ever seen it. That day it was mostly a dark shadow beneath the ship. The Sun lit up one slim crescent. When they reached the sunlit part, Swigert and Haise stared in awe. They got out their cameras and began snapping photos.

Lovell thought about his Apollo 8 mission. How close he had been! If things had gone right, he and Haise would have been preparing to pilot the LM to the surface right now. He felt the sharp sting of disappointment.

In Mission Control, the Maroon Team drank coffee and waited. Kranz and his White Team kept checking and rechecking their calculations. They were determined to make sure absolutely nothing went wrong.

Then, at the expected time, Mission Control picked up the ship's signal again.

Lovell moved around, nervously getting things ready. Haise and Swigert were still glued to their windows. They kept taking photos. Finally, Lovell folded his arms across his chest. He shouted at his crewmates and asked them what they were thinking.

Haise's and Swigert's heads spun toward their commander.

"We have a burn coming up!" cried Lovell. "Is it your intention to participate in it?"

"Jim," said Haise, "this is our last chance to get these shots. Don't you think they're going to want us to bring back some pictures?"

"Hey! If we don't get home, you'll never get them developed!" Lovell shouted. "Now lookit. Let's get the cameras squared away. And let's get set to burn."

Haise and Swigert stowed their cameras and returned to their stations.

They read the spacecraft's position from the LM's computer. The Capcom radioed up the instructions. Haise punched in the data.

The White Team gave everything one final check. Everything looked good. At 8:40 p.m.,

Houston time, the Capcom said, "Jim, you are go for the burn, go for the burn!"

"Roger. Understand. Go for the burn," replied Lovell. He flashed a thumbs-up.

He flipped the switch on Aquarius's control panel. The engine rumbled beneath their feet. After exactly four and a half minutes, the computer shut the engine down.

"That was a good burn, Aquarius," declared the Capcom.

The Mission Control officers stood and cheered. The astronauts had sped up enough to cut ten hours off their trip. They were on their way home! If all went well, they would come down in the Pacific Ocean around noon on Friday, April 17.

Chapter 7

A SQUARE PEG IN A ROUND HOLE

With 230,000 miles still to go, the astronauts had to figure out how to make their small supply of electricity and water last. Even with the time shaved off the trip, Lovell was not sure if there would be enough power to get home. They shut down the computer and turned off all the lights. They turned the heat down to a bitter-cold thirty-eight degrees. As much as possible, they would have to keep the radio off. Hot meals were, of course, out of the question. Every bit of electricity was precious.

With most systems off, they wouldn't need so much water for cooling. Still, they would have to cut back their drinking water to six ounces per day. That's not even one whole glass!

Mission Control knew that oxygen wasn't going to be a problem. However, carbon dioxide was! Every time people breathe out, they let out a gas called carbon dioxide. For humans, this gas is a poison. For that reason, all spacecraft have carbon dioxide scrubbers. The scrubbers have filters that soak up the gas and keep it out of the air. Every so often, the astronauts have to take out a used-up filter and put in a fresh one.

Late Tuesday night, Haise was about to dive into a packet of roast beef and gravy, when Houston asked him to check their carbon dioxide level. The gauge was reading very high. Aquarius had enough filters to last two people fifty-three hours. Now they had three people. They were on their last filter. And it was getting used up fast! Too much carbon dioxide was building up. At this rate, by noon on Wednesday, they would be feeling light-headed and sick. By about 3:00 p.m.—about two days short of their return—they'd all be dead. If they were going to make it home, they would have to think of something quick.

They had extra filters in Odyssey. But Aquarius's scrubber was round. Odyssey's scrubber was square. Those filters wouldn't fit.

Down in Houston, Ed Smylie, the chief of crew systems, made a list of all the odds and ends the astronauts had on the ship—anything that might be useful. He asked his team to figure out how to use these items to make Odyssey's filters fit Aquarius's scrubber. Using scissors, a plastic bag, cardboard, duct tape, and some extra hoses, they cobbled

together a solution. They tested it in the simulator. It didn't look pretty, but it seemed to
work. They wrote down how they built the
thing, step by step.

Early Wednesday morning, Smylie arrived
in the control room with the model tucked
under his arm and the list of instructions in
his hand. The Capcom told the astronauts
what they would need. They hunted around
the ship. Swigert found some duct tape and a
pair of scissors. Haise cut the heavy cardboard
covers off his Lunar Landing Manual. Lovell
opened the storage cabinet at the back of the
LM. He pulled out the long underwear he
and Haise would have worn on the Moon. He
carefully took the underwear out of its plastic
bag and tossed it back in the cabinet. He kept
the plastic with him.

The Capcom read them the instructions.
Step by step, they attached Odyssey's square

filter to the outside of Aquarius's round scrubber. The thing looked so silly, the astronauts nicknamed it the mailbox.

When it was done, they folded their arms and admired their work. "Okay!" declared Swigert. "Our do-it-yourself filter system is complete!"

"Roger," replied the Capcom. "See if air is flowing through it."

Swigert leaned in close and listened. He heard the soft rush of air moving through the filter.

By this time, the carbon dioxide in the cabin was dangerously high. Everyone stared at the gauge in suspense. Slowly but surely, the needle began to fall.

A happy murmur spread through Mission Control.

"I think," said Haise, "I might just finish that roast beef and gravy now."

"I think," said Lovell, "I might just join you."

Chapter 8

COURSE CORRECTION

It wasn't long before the officers in Mission Control grew worried again. Their computers showed that the spacecraft's path was changing. Even a little change would be a disaster by the time they reached Earth. If this continued, Odyssey would not be landing in the Pacific. It would bounce off Earth's atmosphere, like a stone skipping off the surface of a lake.

There was no way around it. They would have to ask the astronauts to fire Aquarius's engine one more time. And they would have to do it soon, because Mission Control could see pressure building up in Aquarius's fuel tank. They expected the valve that controlled the pressure to burst within a few hours. It would make a loud bang when it did. It wouldn't hurt the spacecraft, but a lot of Aquarius's fuel would shoot out. Then there might not be enough fuel left for a course correction.

Swigert and Lovell were in their couches, trying to get some sleep. The flight director told the Capcom not to wake them up with the bad news. The poor guys needed sleep.

Haise was on duty in the LM. The Capcom had just finished warning him about the problem when he heard a loud bang.

Haise radioed down. "I just heard a thump. And I saw a shower of snowflakes come up from below."

Everyone froze. "Okay," said the Capcom. "Understand you got a thump and a few snowflakes."

Haise wondered if it was their fuel valve exploding already. But he knew the LM better than anyone. This was not what it felt like when a valve burst. He tried to stay calm. He wouldn't wake up the commander. Not yet. He would look everything over first.

Mission Control checked the fuel tank's gauge. Pressure was still going up. If the valve had burst, it should be going down. This had to be something else. But what? Then the electrical expert noticed something. The power level on battery two was falling fast!

Had the battery exploded? Aquarius had six batteries. The astronauts needed every one of them to make it home alive. The flight director didn't want to scare them until he knew for sure. He asked his team to check everything again.

Lovell rubbed the sleep from his eyes. He and Swigert popped their heads into the LM.

"Morning," said Haise. "Looks like you finally got some rest."

Lovell looked at his watch. He'd slept for four and a half hours. "Wow! Looks like we did. What's the status of things down here?"

"Well," said Haise, "they've decided on a midcourse burn sometime tonight."

"Mm-hmm," said Lovell.

"Also," Haise said, "looks like we've had a bit of an event."

"An . . . event?"

"A bang and some venting," said Haise.

Lovell reached for his radio headset. He tried hard to sound calm. "Houston, what is our status on venting?"

No one was sure yet. Lovell clenched his jaw. They would just have to wait and see. He went over the plans for the course correction.

Finally, the Capcom told Lovell about the explosion in battery two. But it was probably a small problem. The battery already seemed to be recovering its power.

Lovell still felt uneasy, but they had to get their course correction done soon. If they couldn't get back on course, nothing else would matter. With battery power running lower by the hour, this burn would have to be made without the help of their LM computer.

This time, the Earth would be their marker. Lovell would turn the spacecraft, so he could see the Earth in the center of his window.

"And, Fred, while Jim has the Earth in his window, you should also be able to see the Sun in the telescope," said the Capcom. That would tell them the spaceship was aimed correctly.

"I understand," replied Haise.

Lovell grabbed the joystick and switched on Aquarius's thrusters.

"Houston, Jim has the Earth," Haise said. "And the Sun is in the telescope."

69

"You guys ready to try this?" Lovell asked his crew.

Haise and Swigert nodded.

Lovell held one hand over the start and stop switches. And he wrapped his other hand around the main joystick.

Haise grabbed the other controller.

Throughout the burn, Haise would have to keep the Sun in the center of his telescope's sight. Lovell would be in charge of keeping the Earth in his sight.

Swigert fixed his eyes on his watch. "We'll begin in one minute," he said.

They were all silent.

Swigert began the countdown. "Ten, nine, eight, seven, six, five, four, three, two, one!"

Lovell flicked the start switch. Aquarius's engine came to life once again.

They would have to let the engine burn for exactly fourteen seconds. Swigert began

counting. "One second, two seconds . . ."

Lovell used his joystick to keep the curve of the Earth in the right position. "Holding steady!" he called.

"Five seconds, six seconds . . . ," Swigert continued.

The engine hummed and jiggled.

Lovell held his breath as the Earth jittered and slid to the left.

The Sun bobbled in Haise's telescope.

Haise and Lovell used their controllers. They worked hard to hold their aim.

"Almost there, Fred," said Lovell.

"Fourteen seconds!" cried Swigert.

Lovell hit the stop switch hard. "Shutdown!" he called.

"Shutdown!" echoed Haise.

Aquarius's engine went silent again.

"Houston. Burn complete," said Lovell.

Outside their window, the Earth was about

the size of a dime. As far as Lovell could tell, they seemed to be on target.

In Mission Control, Kranz finally sent his exhausted White Team home for a quick night's sleep. There would be plenty to do the next day, to get ready for splashdown.

Chapter 9

AS COLD AS FROGS
IN A FROZEN POND

At about three o'clock Thursday morning, Haise began to shiver. He felt all tingly and light-headed. When he tried to pee, it burned like crazy. None of them had been drinking much water. So Haise wasn't too surprised.

But Lovell was surprised by how pale his crewmate suddenly looked. "Hey, Freddo. You all right?" he asked.

"Sure," mumbled Haise. "I'm fine. Why?"

"You sure don't look fine, that's why," said Lovell.

"Well, I am."

"You want me to get the thermometer, Fred?" asked Swigert.

"No, don't bother."

"It's no trouble," said Swigert.

"I said I'm fine!"

"Okay, okay," said Swigert. He gave Lovell a doubtful glance.

Clearly Haise was running a fever. Lovell thought about ordering him straight to bed.

Then, from under the LM's floor, came a thump and a hiss. Lovell rushed to his window. He saw a cloud of snowflakes floating upward. The LM's fuel valve had finally burst.

"That," he said, "is the end of our fuel-pressure problem."

"About time," said Haise.

Lovell stared out at the beautiful blue Earth and relaxed.

He didn't have to order his feverish LM

pilot to bed. Haise was already on his way back to Odyssey. But he fell fast asleep before he even got there. His feet floated in the tunnel, and his head hovered over the LM's engine cover. Swigert curled up on the floor. He wrapped a wire around his arm to hold himself in place. Soon he was asleep, too.

At 8:00 Thursday morning, Lovell's crew woke up feeling a little refreshed. Instead of looking pale and gray, Haise now looked rosy pink. Lovell wasn't sure if that meant his LM pilot was getting better or worse. But he decided some breakfast wouldn't hurt.

"Say, Jack," he called, "how do we stand on supplies?"

"Let me check," said Swigert. He opened the bag where he'd stored the food packets from Odyssey. "Not too great, Jim," he said. "Cold soup, cold soup, and . . . looks like some desserts."

"How about running up to the bedroom

and bringing back some food?" asked Lovell.

"No problem," said Swigert.

"You want anything, Freddo?" asked Lovell.

"Sure," said Haise. "How about a few of those hot dogs?"

Swigert floated through the tunnel to the food locker and dug around. At the bottom of the bin, he found the hot dog packets. He grabbed three and swam back, laughing.

"Well, gentlemen," he declared, "I got what you asked for, but I'm not sure you want them."

Lovell took one frost-covered packet from

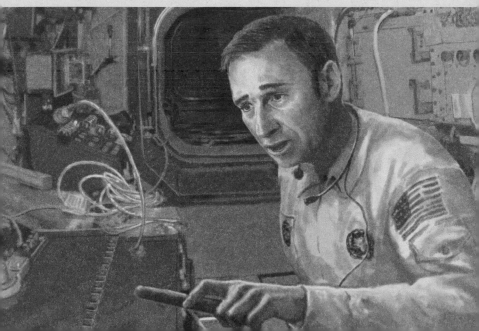

Swigert. Soon he was laughing, too. The hot dog was frozen solid!

Lovell bonked it against the edge of the control panel. "Sounds delicious," he joked.

"Eat hearty!" said Swigert.

Meanwhile, one of the Maroon Team officers had seen something on his control panel that made his stomach sink. The spacecraft's path was changing. Again! No one had any idea what was wrong. The astronauts were in danger of bouncing off the atmosphere. They needed to fire the LM's engine one more time. But now, with most of the fuel gone, that could be impossible.

"Aquarius, Houston!" called the Capcom.

"Go, Houston," Swigert answered.

"Say, fellows, just wanted to let you know that we show you 130,000 miles out now. And you're doing 3,427 miles per hour in a 3,000-mile-per-hour zone."

"Real good," said Swigert.

"There's just one other thing," said the Capcom. He could hardly bear to give them the bad news. They would have to do another burn, about four or five hours before reentry.

"I don't like the sound of this," Lovell said to his crew.

"I'm with you," Haise agreed.

With the fuel gone, the LM's main engine was probably dead. Lovell thought he could use the LM's thrusters to get the spacecraft back on target. But they were small compared to the main engine. He'd have to run them full power for a good half a minute.

Would the little thrusters be able to run that long? He would just have to worry about that when the time came. Now they had to go over the plans for reentry and splashdown. And this was not going to be any ordinary reentry!

Chapter 10

FAREWELL, AQUARIUS, AND WE THANK YOU

The Command Module, Odyssey, was their only hope of getting through Earth's atmosphere safely. They would jettison the SM and the LM and ride home in the CM. But right now, it was as cold as ice in there. Everything was shut down. Normally, it took a whole day to get a Command Module up and running. This time, they had only two hours of electricity to do the job.

The Capcom told Lovell they were working on a plan. It had to be done exactly right, using the least power possible. Ken Mattingly was still feeling fine. And he was still in the simulator. He tried out plan after plan. If the startup took too much power, it had to be scrapped. Time after time, Mattingly sent the engineers back to the drawing board.

Finally, they figured out a way. But there was one terrifying catch. In order to have enough power, the astronauts would have to keep the monitoring system off. That was what helped them keep track of how they were doing. Without it, they wouldn't be able to see their mistakes. They would simply have to get everything right the first time.

Late on Thursday, the Capcom read the instructions up to the ship. It took Swigert almost two hours just to write them down.

"Okay," the Capcom told Swigert. "We did run simulations on all this. So we do think we got all the little surprises ironed out."

"I hope so," said Swigert, "because tomorrow is examination time!"

The doctor had his own worries about the astronauts. They had been working around the clock for more than three days, with hardly any sleep!

Swigert was worried, too. The next morning, once Odyssey was powered up, he would be in charge of jettisoning both the Service Module and the Lunar Module. There were two switches. First, he would flip the SM JETT switch to release the SM. Second, he would flip the LM JETT switch to let go of Aquarius. But stuck in Swigert's mind was one sickening fear. Over and over he saw himself accidentally flipping the wrong switch first, while his crewmates were still aboard Aquarius. In his awful daydream, he watched as his crewmates floated helplessly away.

He couldn't take it anymore. Early Friday

morning, April 17, before he did anything else, he grabbed a small slip of paper and a pen. On the paper he wrote the word "NO." With a piece of duct tape, he fixed the sign over the LM JETT switch.

Lovell looked at the little sign and smiled.

He could hardly believe how cold Odyssey had become. He floated to one of the windows. It was all fogged up. He ran his finger across it. Pearl-sized spheres of water lifted off the window and drifted around his hand.

The warm moisture from the astronauts' breath had collected on the CM's icy-cold walls and windows. Lovell worried that all this water would destroy the electrical connections in his control panel. Everything was made to be waterproof. But just one exposed wire, or one broken seal, and the whole panel could blow out.

In Mission Control, it was time for the

final shift. The White Team took their seats. The other teams pressed into the control room, too. All eyes were glued to the computers as they prepared for one last course correction.

Lovell took a deep breath. There was no time left for worry. He and Haise went back into the LM. At 7:00 a.m., four hours before reentry, Lovell fired Aquarius's thrusters. For thirty seconds, the little engines roared. The spacecraft was back on course!

Mission Control gave Swigert the go-ahead to jettison the Service Module. Swigert flipped the SM JETT switch. The astronauts heard a dull pop and felt a jolt.

Floating back to the CM, Lovell leaned close to his window. He looked for the SM. For a few tense seconds, he didn't see any sign of it. Finally, he spotted it drifting slowly past his window like a huge silver battleship. What he saw left him speechless. He grabbed Haise's arm and pointed. One whole side of their SM had been blasted away. There was a big black hole. And they could see tangled wires hanging loose inside the ship.

"It's really a mess," reported Lovell.

"Okay, Jim," replied the Capcom. "We'd like you to get some pictures." Maybe they would help NASA figure out what had gone wrong.

Swigert already had his camera in hand. Lovell pulled him over toward the window, and he began snapping photos. The astronauts stared at their SM until it was just a tiny glimmering dot in the distance.

"Aquarius, Houston," they heard the Capcom call.

"Go, Houston," said Lovell.

"You're go to start powering up Odyssey."

Lovell nodded to Swigert. The CM pilot began going through the long checklist. One by one, Odyssey's systems came on. At each switch, Lovell braced for the sickening sizzle that would mean one of the systems had blown out. But the only sound he heard was the comforting hum of the spacecraft coming back to life.

Within half an hour, Odyssey was fully up and running. It was finally time to jettison their lifeboat. Aquarius had saved their lives. But now, one hour before reentry, they had to let her go.

Lovell brought a few last items from Aquarius back to Odyssey. "Reporting aboard, skipper," he said to Swigert.

As the CM pilot, Swigert would be in charge of reentry. "Aye, aye," he answered.

"Okay, Houston," he said, "we're ready to proceed with hatch close-up."

"Okay, Jack," said the Capcom. "Did Jim get all the film out of Aquarius?"

Lovell nodded yes.

"Yes," Swigert said. "And we remembered to get Jim out, too."

"Good deal," said the Capcom. "Then what we want you to do is seal the hatch. And you can feel free to release Aquarius."

Lovell sealed the hatch.

Swigert ripped his "NO" off the control panel and crumpled it into a ball. He flipped the LM JETT switch.

The astronauts heard a dull pop. Lovell and Haise gazed out the window. The ship that would have taken them to the Moon drifted slowly away.

"Houston, LM jettison complete," said Swigert.

"Okay, copy that," said the Capcom softly. "Farewell, Aquarius, and we thank you."

"Gentlemen," said Lovell, "we are about to reenter. I suggest you get ready for a ride." He got into his couch and fastened his seat belt.

Swigert and Haise did the same.

"I know all of us here want to thank all you guys for the very fine job you did," Swigert told the Capcom.

"I'll tell you," said the Capcom, "we all had a good time doing it."

In just a few minutes, Odyssey would hit the atmosphere. As the spacecraft moved through the air, the temperature around it would go up to over 5,000 degrees. Odyssey's heat shield had been built to take this kind of heat. But was it still in one piece? Had the explosions damaged it? There was no way to know.

For four minutes, while Odyssey reached its highest temperature, all radio contact would be lost. If Mission Control could hear the astronauts' voices again after four minutes, they'd know the heat shield had done its job. If not, they'd know their crew had died a fiery death.

Chapter 11

WELCOME HOME

The White Team officers checked their control panels. They gave Flight Director Kranz their thumbs-ups. "Odyssey, Houston," said the Capcom. "We just had one last time around the room, and everyone says you're looking great. We'll have loss of signal in about half a minute. Welcome home."

"Thank you," said Swigert.

The astronauts watched as the air began to glow pink outside their windows. Then it turned orange. And then bright red! They saw fiery flakes from the heat shield zooming past. As Odyssey warmed up, the droplets of water on the walls and windows began to fall on them. It was raining inside the spacecraft.

The radio crackled.

In Mission Control, everyone listened to the static and watched the clock. No one said a word.

Three minutes.

Four minutes.

"All right," Kranz told the Capcom, "advise the crew we're standing by."

"Odyssey, Houston standing by, over," radioed the Capcom.

They heard nothing but static.

"Odyssey, Houston standing by," repeated the Capcom.

Fifteen seconds went by.

Nothing.

Thirty more seconds.

Still no reply.

The officers stared at their computer screens.

Three more seconds.

Finally, they heard what sounded like a slight wobble in the static.

"Okay, Joe!"

It was Swigert's voice!

The Capcom closed his eyes and took a deep breath. The flight director pumped his fist in the air. Everyone jumped from their chairs and began hugging one another. The astronauts had made it.

"Okay," replied the Capcom. "We read you, Jack."

Lovell and his crew heard Odyssey's first set of parachutes open. With exact timing, those chutes were jettisoned, and the three main parachutes opened up. The astronauts felt a bump as their speed dropped to only twenty miles per hour.

Normally, Apollo CMs landed in the middle of the Pacific Ocean. But this flight was far from normal! After the second burn, Mission Control knew that Odyssey would land in the southern Pacific Ocean. A U.S. Navy ship, the *Two Jima*, had headed in that direction right away.

For days, a hurricane had been threatening the area. On the morning of landing day, though, the weather was looking good. The sailors on the *Two Jima* listened in on NASA's radio communications. Standing on deck, the recovery team leader searched the sky.

Suddenly a sailor cried, "There it is!"

The team leader turned. He spotted it, too!

A news reporter turned his camera in that direction. In Mission Control, they saw Odyssey appear on their main TV screen. The spacecraft was sailing down under its three giant orange and white parachutes.

All around the world, millions of people stopped what they were doing. They gathered around any television that was nearby. They saw the same beautiful image.

"Odyssey, Houston," said the Capcom.

"Got you on television, babe!"

"Roger," replied Swigert.

"Hang on," said Lovell to his crewmates. If this landing was like Apollo 8's, they were in for a real jolt. He grabbed the edges of his couch. Swigert and Haise did the same.

Thirty seconds later, Odyssey splashed down in the water. The landing was very gentle. Lovell smiled in surprise.

"Fellows," he said. "We're home."

EPILOGUE

Within minutes, a navy helicopter came to pick up the astronauts. It landed on the deck of the *Iwo Jima*, and the exhausted astronauts climbed out. The ship's doctor gave them checkups. They were woozy from lack of water, and they had lost a lot of weight. The doctor gave Haise medicine for his fever.

That evening they enjoyed a feast of shrimp, prime rib, salad, and lobster. They guzzled big mugs of water and orange juice. The next day, they were flown to Hawaii. The president of the United States, Richard M. Nixon, and the astronauts' families were there to meet them.

NASA studied Swigert's photos of the damaged Service Module. They showed that oxygen tank two had been the problem. The tank's temperature controller had been broken. Before the trip, the small heater inside the tank had overheated. This burned off the protective covering on some of the tank's wires. When Swigert switched on the fan to give the oxygen a stir, sparks flew from the bare wires and the oxygen exploded.

Apollo 14 was fitted with better temperature controllers and more heavily covered wires. Eight months later, it was ready to fly. Apollos 14 through 17 were successful missions. In all, twenty-four humans have flown to the Moon, and twelve have walked on it.

THE STORY BEHIND THE STORY

APOLLO 13

WHAT HAPPENED NEXT?

Jim Lovell worked for NASA until 1973. He wrote a book about Apollo 13 that later became a famous movie. He even got to play a small role! Jack Swigert retired from NASA in 1973. He ran for Congress in his home state of Colorado. Fred Haise worked on NASA's space shuttle program in the 1970s. He left

NASA in 1979 but went on to work as a test pilot for many years. Ken Mattingly never did get German measles. He finally got his chance to go to the Moon in 1972, on Apollo 16.

SATURN V ROCKETS

The Saturn V rockets were built in the Vertical Assembly Building, one of the largest buildings ever constructed. It was only three and a half miles away from the launch-pad. But how do you move a gigantic rocket? By using a steel-treaded 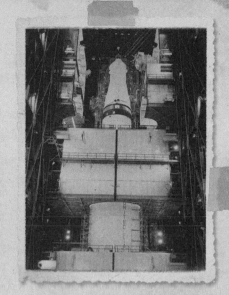 tractor called the crawler. It was 131 feet long and 113 feet wide and weighed almost six million pounds.

Once the rocket was loaded onto the crawler, the driver could crank it up to a top speed of *one mile per hour*!

HOW DO YOU GO TO THE BATHROOM IN SPACE?

The Apollo space suits were equipped with a urine catcher. Astronaut Pete Conrad joked that he might not have been the first man to walk on the Moon, but he was the first person to pee in his pants on the Moon. The urine catcher in his suit made that possible.

When the astronauts were not in their space suits, they could hook themselves up to a tube with a short hose that led to a bag. When their bags were full, they emptied them through a nozzle that shot the urine into space.

Pooping in space was more difficult. The poop went straight into a plastic bag, which the astronauts had to tape to their butts. In zero gravity, getting the poop to stay in the bag was sometimes a problem! Some of the Apollo astronauts said that pooping in space was the absolute worst part of their trip. The whole process, from start to cleanup, took anywhere from thirty to forty-five minutes! NASA engineers came up with better devices for later missions.

MASS VS. WEIGHT

Whether you are on the Earth, on the Moon, or anyplace in the universe, the amount of material in your body remains the same. That is your mass. Your weight, on the other hand, depends on gravity. On the Moon, the gravity is one-sixth that of Earth. So, if you weigh ninety pounds on Earth, you would weigh only fifteen pounds on the Moon.

PLACES TO VISIT

- **Kansas Cosmosphere and Space Center, Hutchinson.** See the Command Module, Odyssey.
- **Kennedy Space Center, Cape Canaveral, Florida.** Learn more about NASA and see the Saturn V rocket.
- **National Air and Space Museum, Washington, D.C.** Learn more about NASA and space flight.
- **Space Center Houston.** See the Mission Control room and other Apollo 13 artifacts.

APOLLO 13

Look for the numbers on the map to follow Lovell, Haise, and Swigert on their adventure.

1. Liftoff!
2. After orbiting Earth three times, the spacecraft is "GO for TLI."

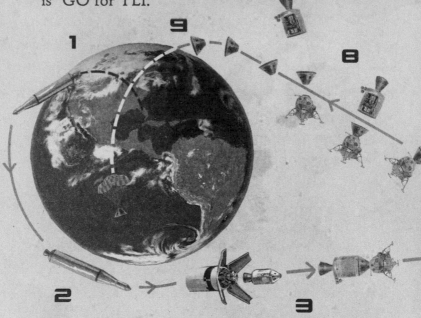

3. The astronauts attach the LM to the CM.
4. *BANG!* The astronauts hear and feel a big explosion. They must move to the LM.

5. Radio contact is lost on the dark side of the Moon.
6. The astronauts must use the LM's engine.
7. The spacecraft goes off course twice! The astronauts must re-aim the spacecraft.
8. Swigert jettisons the SM and LM.
9. The CM enters Earth's atmosphere. Splashdown!

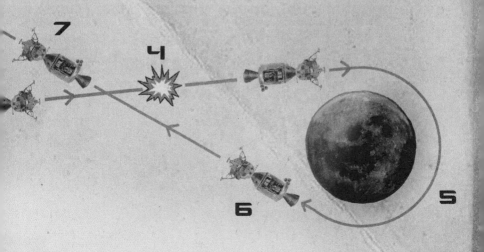

ACKNOWLEDGMENTS

Special thanks to my wonderful editors Jennifer Arena and Paula Sadler, copy editor Katie Cicatelli-Kuc, and designers Jason Zamajtuk and Ginny Chu, as well as the helpful curators and docents at the USS *Hornet* Museum and the Chabot Space and Science Center, and Jim Remar at the Kansas Cosmosphere and Space Center.

This book couldn't have been written without Jim Lovell and Jeffrey Kluger's exciting and detailed account of the mission, *Lost Moon*, and NASA's complete "Apollo 13 Technical Air-to-Ground Voice Transcription," which can be read online at www.hq.nasa.gov/alsj /a13/AS13_TEC.PDF.

ABOUT THE AUTHOR

Kathleen Weidner Zoehfeld vividly remembers growing up during the Space Age. She watched the Apollo 11 launch on TV and memorized the names and faces of all the NASA astronauts. At age ten, if you asked her what she wanted to be when she grew up, she said, "An astronaut, of course!"

When she grew up, she became a writer and editor, not an astronaut. But some of her favorite books to edit have been about space travel and astronomy. She has written more than sixty books for young readers, including three other Stepping Stones, *Fossil Fever, The Curse of King Tut's Mummy,* and *Finding the First T. Rex.*

She's still hoping for a chance to travel in outer space. In the meantime, she enjoys traveling through time by volunteering at her local natural history museum and learning about the fossil life of the past.

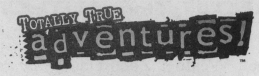

Crack! An edge of ice split off and dropped into the deep dark hole. Hillary fell. He tried to slow himself by jamming his boots into the icy wall.

"Tenzing!" he shouted. "Tenzing!"

In a flash, Tenzing plunged his ice ax into the snow. He wrapped his rope around the ax to hold it steady. Then he threw himself on the ground, to anchor the rope even more.

The rope tightened. Hillary jerked to a stop. He was fifteen feet down, far into the crack of ice. Bit by bit, he pulled himself up. His gloves were torn, and his body was bruised. But he was alive.